a child walks in the dark

Darren C. Demaree

Harbor Editions
Small Harbor Publishing

Cover art by Laura Page
Cover design by Claire Eder
Book layout by Allison Blevins and Hannah Martin
Book editing by Callista Buchen

A CHILD WALKS IN THE DARK
DARREN C. DEMAREE
ISBN 978-1-7359090-7-3
Harbor Editions,
an imprint of Small Harbor Publishing

For my family—

CONTENTS

a child walks in the dark

[THOSE JUNK PLUMS]

i told my children those junk plums left at the bottom of the grocery bag were not perfect when we put them in the bag but they were on sale and good enough for a family that doesn't get many plums now that they are mangled and losing their juice to the bottom of the thin green bag i struggled so mightily to remove from the dispenser we are still going to cup their mangled flesh in our hands we are still going to eat them however inelegant that might be we are going to pour the remnants into a tiny cup we are going to celebrate the fact that there is still fruit in this world that won't always be the case

[SUMMER IS OPEN]

i told my son summer is open and he refused to wear clothes for three months it was difficult most of the time but i've never been prouder each flex and dance of his body was a goddamn show for all of the neighbors and he smiled and laughed and touched his penis way too often in front of the salespeople that i would always invite back to the house another time but would never return and i know in a year or two he will learn embarrassment from someone but it will not be from me

[IF YOU WANT TO READ ALL OF THE BOOKS]

i told my daughter if you want to read all of the books the best thing to do is to memorize one of them and then slowly misremember the names of all of the characters learn many languages and translate the text in your mind many times over after a while the names will all disappear the pronouns will fold into each other the actions will simplify the descriptions will become your own eventually you've been living the all-story and the library will feel exactly like a church

[IF THEY EVER FIND THEMSELVES STRAPPED TO THE MAST]

i told my children if they ever find themselves strapped to the mast of a ship that is headed into water they do not desire they should ignore the ocean they should break free they should find the gun powder they should set it ablaze they should jump overboard and swim so far so quickly that they never hear the screams of their captors they're my children i've taught them to swim for this reason i've been treading water next to wreckage and bodies of the ship i was once tied to i'm hopeful that one of the children will make it to shore our family name has been at sea for a century

[ONE CANDLE]

i told my son one candle is a town gone missing a town dragged behind
the poet's car to become a scene where there is too much gravel and
you boy lovely boy i'm going to need you to tie the citizens of jelloway
to our car because i need to take a shot at writing some midwestern
gothic that has no chance of flight something where the retention
pond is just deep enough to be a distraction while i run with the havoc
these people are most accustomed to you can hold the actual candle
stand back

[THERE IS A SMALL SONG]

i told my daughter there is a small song a loose skin a lip bend an obvious note or two in every day that could be folded into the minutes but you choose to roll around your tongue and release into the echo that always returns to tease your tongue in the best of life's inelegant displays don't tell me what you call it just promise me you'll be as playful with the world as it is with you that you'll sing nonsense amidst the nonsense and smile because it's all yours

[THE PIPES IN THE RAIN]

i told my daughter the pipes in the rain are bear claws that can only attempt to pool the rain but can never keep it long enough to warp the metal even slightly so if she wants to wear her own indentation into the framework of the world she will need to learn how to drink the ocean to bring the ocean to the fields and build her castle out of salt of course of course of course that thirsty bear can live in your castle children are with the deer and the forest the bear always that's why they are always willing to defy the elemental nature of things because they are small enough and see well enough that they can rearrange the atomic structure of all things they can pluck the fantasy to drag it into the real world and i can barely change how i order my coffee which is why i spend all of my time listening to her voice get louder more confident

[THE ROOTS HAVE RISEN UP AWAY FROM THE TRUNK]

i told my children the roots have risen up away from the trunk and like your brain seeps the tree's structure seeps as well and searches and keeps searching even in the spring because the nourishment doesn't come from the good black or the tall blue visiting it comes from growing until you bump your head on the ceiling until you are a giant in your own world and that will be the first part of your lives the second the third the fourth and the fifth will be learning how important it is to lower yourself to make yourself a ramp to feed the rising of the people around you that first decided all these roots were a good thing

[THERE IS ENOUGH YOUTH]

i told my son there is enough youth in you for all of us of course you can paint the wall with your helmet on while you stand on the bookshelf and shout-sing your favorite lines from under pressure which you learned from an animated movie where a koala sacrifices his whole past for one night of good art which yields him ruin and more art and you boy i don't know why you got naked to do all of this but i suppose it does make sense to me on an elemental level son are you the new element some sort of fleshy stone that hums at a rhythm this family as not yet known yes yes yes you're right david bowie and queen it's all so incredible

[THE DARK GETS COLD]

i told my daughter the dark gets cold but that doesn't mean you have to pull the eyes out of the dead fish you've been given it doesn't mean you have to eat the fish you and the fish have both existed in a time that held little warmth and that time will change as all times change and i hope you never forget what it felt like to have your hand hover over death's reminder that you are more than any pale gesture the world chooses to make

[A MASK OR TWO]

i told my children a mask or two is flesh enough to keep your bones out of the fire and i love all of the people you will try and fail to be and i love all of the lies you will tell yourself and i love you for lying to me about who you are and want to be as long as you are always searching for that person i will say all of the names you give yourself as long as you are living i will hold every incarnation of your world as part of my own

[THE WORDS AGAIN]

i told my children the words again that i could tell them which was all the words including the profanity which can be like a deep fucking breath when you need it to be and they had no interest in those words or in most of my words but they could tell i was trying to give them a gift and they remembered how much time i took trying to give it to them and then i was done and nobody could tell anybody anything anymore but we loved each other in that you can't really explain in primary colors sort of way and they knew the darkness and the light and they jumped rope with that with an agility i've never found they weren't shocked or hopeful they just made a path towards the best ending they could they moved forward with their bodies with their hearts with their songs they sang out loud all of the time

[IT'S ONE DEFEAT AT A TIME]

i told my daughter it's one defeat at a time this holy darkness this
january belief system of yours but if you want most of all to believe in
one death i find no fault in that in the narrowing of your eyes in an
attempt to blur the world into order or beauty but there have been
billions of deaths already most of them lives preempted in some way
so maybe as you grow older you might consider joining me in
remembering that it takes billions of deaths to create a god and only
one life really lived and remembered to cement the place of all
humanity

[THE SELF-REMOVAL]

i told my son the self-removal is an acceptance of your own refraction you will become six men in sixteen different worlds and you can't possibly police all of them so become none of them be an agent for every person in every world that needs you keep your hands warm keep your shoulders loose forget what your face looks like say i love without a name attached embrace that none of this is nonsense defend your right to be a tide only destroy nothing but your own ego

[THE CONTROL OF THE BIRD]

i told my daughter the control of the bird is a soft balling of freedom thrown back into the air one more time and she should never once discount flight happening right in front of her because that could be the last time it happens and it's a long shot that hollow bones will last much longer in a world that has bet heavy on the idea that it can trap the sun

[THERE'S NO PLACE TO GO]

i told my children there's no place to go wild that isn't coated in sea-top so they should head to the sea and find out exactly what it is they can get away with or give away if they so desire most of desire has ended or began near the tides it's horribly beautiful that way so we go every year so i can tell my children there's no place to go where they can be complete and the acceptance of that should open them up to the idea that though they are not the ocean they are of the ocean and they cannot be worn down by what happens on this rock

[A TETHERED GOAT]

i told my daughter a tethered goat is a warning that the balance of the
scene is off that there is a hope against the danger that there is a
danger that there is not enough freedom for her to stay there long at all
and when she tries to free the goat before she frees herself she invites
the danger to meet her face-to-face and maybe just maybe that is the
kind of girl she wants to become and when i said those last words she
showed me two fists and a fullness i'd never found in myself and i
wondered out loud if i might have been the goat the whole time

[YOU'RE A WITCH]

i told my son you're a witch if you want to be but do your best to be a good witch and if you find the right dark magic please don't tell me about it show me

[YOU CAN REACH ME]

i told my son you can reach me i am not the weather the same way my father was the weather i am not mystery or storm or the perfect day apology for the storm you can reach me i am willing to be shaken i used to be shaken all of the time you you you son you can reach me i have built a table too small to eat at so that we can sit there and hold no pursuit other than me what do you need

[THE FIELDS TOWARDS YOU]

i told my son the field moves towards you and it doesn't matter if you're crop or the shit crop needs the field will take you if you let the bonfire die down with a circle of people around it the field will find you son and take you with it because your father deserved to be taken for all of those empty two-liter bottles of whiskey and ginger ale yet i was never planted the way fate or the field had wanted so they'll both be coming for you so if you find yourself just far enough off the two-lane to get away with almost anything watch yourself because the entire planet earth is a revenge story and you're already a part of it

[THAT LITTLE GHOST]

i told my son that the little host that cold sighing you feel when you walk into your room is actually the air conditioning unit i dragged up there to keep you cool in the summer oh no there is a ghost up there her lover used to knock on our door because he lived across the street and had dementia and kept forgetting he had decided to stay with his wife those many years ago so she's up there still leaning on the cape cod slant of the house she had built before she knew what would happen if you loved that which existed directly out your front door she's up there but she just wants stay there and look out the window maybe you could decide to pray one night you could pray for her or just say the word love over and over again with your warm breath

[IT WON'T EXPLODE]

i told my children it won't explode the world the world the world will
go on shock by shock until there is one grid for the living and one grid
for the dead there will be an actual heaven and we will finally admit it is
life it is life it is life and the pain we consider to be all too human is just
human enough for the context of absolute joy

[ON THIS PLANE]

i told my daughter on this plane of existence she is newer than sorrow and older than the gate to sorrow so her life must be inelegant enough to have not fit through that opening yet so i gave her the hose and pointed her to the dry dirt in our backyard and asked her to make a mess to love the mess and carry it with her always it's much better to be unacceptable in most of the adult world

[YOU ARE THE STORM]

i told my daughter you are the storm clapping i can smell your electricity coming to life please tell me which cities to avoid when you decide the real revolution is starting because when i told you our president was trying to hurt the planet you broke a lamp you're seven so i thought that was a bit extreme but there was no punishment there will be no punishment you are the punishment for everyone that gets in the way of a thriving earth and it's my job to stay out of your way

[THE NOISE RIPENS]

i told my son the noise ripens in your gut all you have to do is open your mouth wide enough to birth the field that can become the crop that will lift your words high enough to have a chance to be stumbled upon by a party that is searching or the almost destruction of youth and willing to settle for the shape of the story you give them so good luck son because this next ohio is all yours

[ALL OF THE COSTUMES]

i told my son all of the costumes you want to wear are fine with me i don't even care if you become the characters you dress as and i don't care that you change your clothes six times a day you don't have to escape the lion if you're dressed as a lion you don't have to rely on batman if you are batman hell i was a whiskey bottle for twelve years you should have seen how drunk i was able to stay with a full liter of canadian club in my person son i think i like your way better at least your way won't cut up your mother if everything shatters in this house again

[THE FLOWERS MAY GROW]

i told my son the flowers may grow all around you but that doesn't mean you're part of a garden so what so what so what isn't it all so lovely walk walk walk like you know the difference between the bloom and the crop consume gently my boy

[DIGGING IN THE SAND]

i told my children digging in the sand will strengthen your hands but nothing built without a feathering will rise above the coming storms so you'd be best served to stick tomato chunks in your fists and raise them towards the sky once the juice reaches your chest you will know whether you need to run

[ABOUT THE EVENING FLAME]

i told my children about the evening flame about the different world that is heated by it about the reconnaissance that finds good focus once the sun goes about how often there are crowds of people huddled under one light bulb huddled under one diagnosis that whistles through the ears of the sleeping folk and they my children are welcome to sleep as long as they'd like to but if they ever find themselves showering in the low wattage they should know that everyone is watching and some of the watchers want nothing more than to write down the age the gender the race and the sexuality of every person that bothers to dance through the stillness

[AN ORANGE FRUIT BOWL]

i told my daughter an orange fruit bowl is useless if there is no fruit in the bowl and she told me that was exactly what was wrong with boys

[SO VERY SOON]

i told my daughter so very soon you will see your body for the first time since you were born and that reflection will mean something to you please know how beautiful you are please know it was your face i saw recurring when i was in rehab please know you are beautiful enough for me to be the opposite of the person i was born to be

[COLLARBONES]

i told my daughter collarbones are the gates you should never tear down but if you come across a government building outside of your own body you should pull on that motherfucker until it falls down behind you how i will admire your arms when they reach through the iron to cast it aside how i will understand when you pause to watch your sisters rush past you into the courtyard the broken pieces of you that stand next to this new world will speak plainly to the ultimate love i feel when you squint your eyes at the problems of this world

[DRINKING WHERE THE ANIMALS DRINK]

i told my son drinking where the animals drink is a lovely picture but once you're with the deer you're with the deer forever i know this as i am with the deer now

[BY THE RIVER]

i told my children by the river we can replace ourselves we can send ourselves down the finishing angle of the land's veins we can return to the heart we can breathe deep enough to cycle every identity we've ever had and i encourage you to try on a few people before we leave the flood zone then once we get past the sandbags you can push the whole of the landscape beneath three feet of whatever you've become

[A SIMPLE SCREAM]

for Anselm Berrigan

i told my son a simple scream can cut the song in half can frame a page without an illustration can make us all artists by granting the premise that since we are each our own world then we are all the caretakers of each world's art but since in some worlds bombs are art we must prepare ourselves for art to kill a whole lot of people because the violence of such a separating force will inevitably reach the children and i told my son we are all targets but we're also alone together and willing to fill as many pages that are left blank by the anti-swallowing of a whole city block

[CREATION MYTHS]

i told my daughter creation myths are dance music every one of them is a techno beat that works best with good drugs and when she asked me about good drugs i started to talk about god again and i felt very clever about what i had just done there and i bobbed my head to the strobe of my own understanding which she will remember when she chooses a god over her own father

[A BREAK BETWEEN ACTS]

i told my son a break between acts is a myth there is one act and son you're in it you should dance or something

[LET IT GO]

i told my children let it go is an awful song that they should hold on to
everything until they become the mountain royalty has to deal with

[NOT EVERY DARK OUTLINE IS A SHORE]

i told my children not every dark outline is shore but you're swimmers so that shouldn't matter as much as how strong you are that shouldn't matter if shock by shock you transfer the energy the spark you were somehow born with amidst all these changing tides besides no one in your family has ever stood on the beach before so you should go wide with your body float when you need to and rise quickly if it looks like the whole ocean is coming for you

[NOT FAR OFF]

i told my children not far off for you are the bodies we never bury the victims and the guilty and the innocent caught and shot down by the police their blood a river that never browns their faces consumed by the siblings of the life they had wanted and children you will find yourselves in the same bullet-lane of america and though you know none of those bullets will come from me there is little aiming in this world and a whole lot random and even more guns and even more guns and even more guns and even more guns

[SHE IS ENOUGH TO BREAK OPEN ANY ATOM]

i told my daughter she is enough to break open any atom but i'm sure she'll figure out a way to peel back the world like a clementine that she'll floss her teeth with the white veins of the world that she'll get to choose whether or not the moon is ours forever or just the cap of the acorn that is blown off when gravity gives in to the rest of the universe i told my daughter she could ride the ocean whenever she pleases and she responded that might be the ocean and i have yet to argue with her about that

[GALORE]

i told my daughter galore is my favorite word it used to be ergo but that
was when i was drinking all of the time now my favorite word is galore
and she should live a life full of galore love galore dessert galore
regrets galore ashes galore happy choirs sad choirs sexy black
mourning black fabrics galore she should live a story that never ends so
that when it does end she is given exits galore

[A POCKETFUL OF FIRE]

i told my son a pocketful of fire would turn him into an urn and he
decided to take his pants off and leave them in the middle of the road
and i thought that might be protest and after he took the rest of his
clothes off to pose in front of the rest of ohio i knew it was protest
and that he had palmed the fire anyway because he's my son and he
knows how to put on a show and keep the ounces of sun i gave him
for the actual fight

[IF YOU EVER FIND YOURSELF PART OF THE LANDSCAPE]

i told my daughter if you ever find yourself part of the landscape run run run run run or stay and burn that painting down to the frame landscapes always treat women like livestock

[IF YOU EVER FIND YOURSELF PART OF THE LANDSCAPE]

i told my son if you ever find yourself part of the landscape you should make a home there generate a little narrative you can wrap your world around there skate swim sing long to be crop but never become crop be harvested willingly when the mountain comes to the valley shout to echo

[EACH BULLET]

i told my children each bullet is a promise to at least one person that they will die in a puddle that they will be turned into the sky and the fireball that consumes it that each bullet is a solar flare that laps up whole families with each slight burst that each bullet can swallow the firmament whole

[THAT COAL]

i told my children that coal was a mountain fever that men had ridden the blood of the mountain into the valley and then flooded the valley to that they could pick up the paychecks off the dead bodies that floated there and those bodies that felt the rush of cool water before they expired they were the lucky ones and that coal in america is our fourth saddest slaughter story but for some reason very few people have had to answer for the body count so if they want to if they really want to my children are welcome to tell anybody that manages or owns coal to fuck right off because language is important and i don't want them wasting those words on anybody that doesn't deserve it

[THE AMPUTATION DOESN'T MEAN WHAT YOU THINK IT DOES]

i told my children the amputation doesn't mean what you think it does the same thing twice never happens the dreaming is real the myth is the belief in the dream the lesson is that the sea level of where you live is very important unless you are fearless or unless you can swim the rest of the glistening comes from how reality can fold itself and children if you ever understand anything about physics you'll know how important it is to lose all phantom feelings for this world the loss the loss comes with not remembering how this flailing began center mass

[WHAT PLEASURE]

i told my children what pleasure is to you will dictate how much flesh
of the bloom you pull out with your teeth what if i can swallow it
whole what if i can swallow it whole what if i can swallow it whole
they asked and i told them both that was boring and fascist but good
for them i suppose

[IF YOU WANT TO BE A BALLPLAYER]

i told my daughter if you want to be a ballplayer you will need to learn how needless it is to have a pristine body because they never get all the rocks out of the field and this game is dull and pointless if you don't throw yourself into the grass like it's the ocean and i know you love the ocean the same way your mother does but she was never a ballplayer because her parents gave her the ocean i don't have that kind of money so you will need to treat each game like the tide

[IN A WORLD I'VE NEVER SEEN]

i told my son in a world i've never seen there is a flawless heart that beats to circle the world with oxygenated love and it is lovely and useless in the world i've seen but that heart that heart that heart could be something akin to adrenaline something that keeps the world i've seen wondering about its own breath and son dear son ornery boy as long as you wonder and breathe then you will have kept up the bargain you made when you could breathe through the waters of almost existence and this this this existence you can imagine it to be anything you want it to be as long as you keep your hands to yourself

[HER BODY]

i told my daughter her body is no narrative her body is an ocean and a moon and there is no freckle no nail no strand of hair that she is not in charge of and that means that if we do this right she will continue the proper revolution that leads to her lifting up the whole of our government in her hands and shaking them the way they so badly want to shake her and if she doesn't stop until their tongues are flags in the wind then that is her decision because i'm not raising an american or an ohioan i'm raising a girl that will become a woman and she will know her body is whatever the fuck she decides it is and any sail that any person tries to stick in her back to change her path will be burned in a pile i give her when she no longer needs me to write such things

[CALL IT WHAT YOU WILL]

i told my children call it what you will the night is a boat without shoreline we all wake up adrift unheard loved only by our own skin no footprints circling us drowned wolves floating all around the rain held as forgiveness for what we do not know and that is a good night with good sleep in a bed that is paid off in a house that will never be owned by anyone other than the bank and if you're truly blessed there will be other boats slowly rocking near your own but never ask for another to stand up until they are ready occasionally a wolf is revived by the mist by the sun by the plot

[A SINGLE CREATURE]

i told my children a single creature can scream but it takes a chorus to gather the wolves to scent the mountain ridge to make the branches thread enough to canopy the revolution so they should make plenty of friends that want to find nature to be with nature and then attack every wall that confronts nature

[THE COLD BLUE MOON]

i told my daughter the cold blue moon could hold her if she wanted it
to but since we are already drag the past behind us it would be better if
she left the future alone for a little while if she watched the horses at
the county fair without trying to ride one of them if she reached up
into the sky to tease her own reflection in the clouds leave the
depressions in the mood depressed because even though she is
probably the answer to every query the moon has yet to ask for her and
i'd like her to remain seven and unimportant to the firmament a little
bit longer

[WHAT I LIKE TO HIDE]

i told my son what i like to hide are the reasons i have to hide so many things from him and he told me he thought that was stupid and because he was right i let him say it four times in a row before i moved him to counting to one hundred by fives something he loves to do and while he did this i thought about how one day he will wake up and be able to frame me completely so i went ahead and told him i was an alcoholic and he just kept on counting to one hundred by fives and i joined him until we got to ninety and then i let him finish things all by himself

[NOT THE DEAD BOY ON THE NEWS]

i told my son that he was not the dead boy on the news that they were together that they are together that sometimes bombs go off inside the hearts of little boys that sometimes those boys are born with bombs inside their hearts that sometimes adults put bombs inside the hearts of little boys and when he asked me if there was a bomb inside of his heart i lied to him many times i lied to him many times i told him that sometimes it matters how many fingers you have on each hand and sometimes that couldn't matter less and sometimes the best thing is to look down upon your body and imagine the ticking as a gift

[YOU SHOULD TELL ME NOW THAT YOU DON'T CARE]

i told my children you should tell me now that you don't care that you're going to be fire-starters and con artists and painters that you will only need me for alibis so i can let you know now that i'm your man and if this is going to be my adventure to follow you and watch your synapses fire quickly all of the time fire incorrectly and beautifully all of the time then i am in don't hurt children don't steal from poor folks do not plagiarize anything ever do you hear me other than that i'm willing to do a couple of years in jail if it means you will get to dance around this universe like you've figured something out

[YOU MIGHT CHOOSE TO READ THESE POEMS]

i told my children you might choose to read these poems in the bareness and anxiety of your young adulthood while you search for me in the thousands and thousands of poems I have written so that i could explore so that i could explain so that i could hide and lie about some small terribleness and it gives me endless joy that you will find me here right here right now as bare as you are but feeling no anxiety at all because i am with my children in some small way in the future when i love you even more than i already do because that's how real love works it grows with the epic it encircles the epic until you cannot tell why or how any of this began but you know you know you know that if there is such a thing as a soul it exists to be buoyed by moments like this

ACKNOWLEDGMENTS

Bookends Review "[you can reach me]"

Diode "[a single creature]," "[the cold blue moon]," and "[what i like to hide]"

Into the Void "[not the dead boy in the news]"

Leveler "[there's no place to go]"

Lotus-Eater "[a tethered goat]"

Midway Journal "[about the flower]"

Origins "[the noise ripens]," "[each bullet]," and "[the control of the bird]"

Otoliths "[digging in the sand]," "[the pipes in the rain]," and "[a simple scream]"

RavensPerch "[the flowers may grow]," "[a mask or two]," and "[the dark gets cold]"

Red Wolf "[drinking where the animals drink]," "[an orange fruit bowl]," and "[what pleasure]"

Review Americana "[it won't explode]" and "[so very soon]"

Rise Up Review "[those junk plums]"

Smoky Blue Literary and Arts Magazine "[that little ghost]"

Split Lip Magazine "[on this plane]" and "[more than other songs]"

Streetlight "[all the costumes]" and "[the roots have risen away from the trunk]"

tenderness, yea "[the field moves towards you]" and "[you are the storm]"

Tipton Poetry Journal "[if they ever find themselves strapped to the mast]"

Whale Road Review "[you might choose to read these poems]"

Darren C. Demaree grew up in Mount Vernon, Ohio. He is a graduate of the College of Wooster, Miami University, and Kent State University. He is the recipient of a 2018 Ohio Arts Council Individual Excellence Award, the Louise Bogan Award from Trio House Press, and the Nancy Dew Taylor Award from Emrys Journal. He is the Editor-in-chief of the *Best of the Net Anthology* and Managing Editor of *Ovenbird Poetry*. He is currently working in the Columbus Metropolitan Library system, and living in Columbus, Ohio, with his wife and children. *a child walks in the dark* is his sixteenth full-length collection of poetry.

Made in the USA
Monee, IL
09 March 2025

13461174R00046